The Way It Feels Sometimes

Painted by Paula S. Wallace

*For Ronda Fincher and Patty Martin
and the many who found hope
in their deepest sorrow.*

Life is mostly froth and bubble.
Two things stand like stone:
Kindness in another's trouble,
Courage in your own.

Adam Lindsay Gordon
from *Ye Wearie Wayfarer*

When Corky gets the blues,
she learns that sometimes,
there are no words.

This is her journey.

This is the way
it feels sometimes.

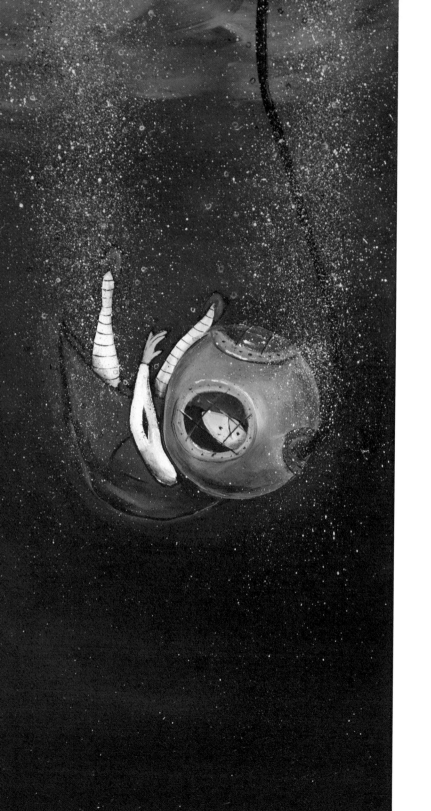

Thrown in,

the blahs.

The long climb,

anger and frustration.

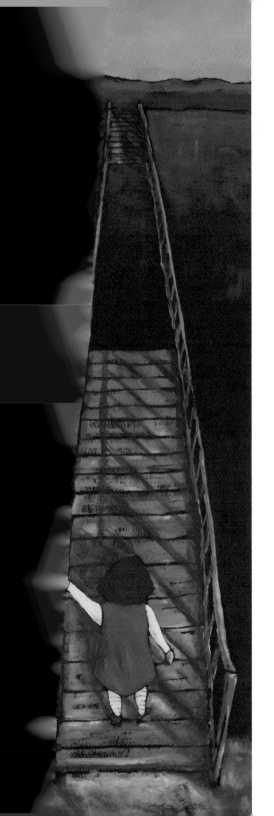

No way to the
other side.

The deepest hole,

the empty chair.

The night will never stay,
The night will still go by,
Though with a million stars
You pin it to the sky;
Though you bind it with a blowing wind
And buckle it with the moon,
The night will slip away
Like sorrow or a tune.

Eleanor Farjeon
from *Poems for Children*

Adrift,

lost,

wanting a sign.

"Hope" is the thing with feathers—
That perches in the soul—
And sings the tune without the words—
And never stops—at all—

And sweetest—in the Gale—is heard—
And sore must be the storm—
That could abash the little Bird
That kept so many warm—

I've heard it in the chillest land—
And on the strangest Sea—
Yet, never, in Extremity,
It asked a crumb—of Me.

Emily Dickinson
Hope is a Thing with Feathers (314)

Even a small light will shine in the darkness.

Studio 100 Productions
paulawallacefineart.com

The book is the illustrator's concept for a series exploring grief and hope.
Many thanks to Terry Koopman at Photographics in Omaha, Nebraska, who makes the work possible through his services and good cheer, and to Jeffrey Hahn at Paradigm Creative Media, Inc. of Omaha who assisted with the layout.

A thousand thanks to Lisa, Rachel, and the Concierge Marketing team and to the Omaha Creative Institute's Community Supported Art program.

10 9 8 7 6 5 4

CPSIA information can be obtained at www.ICGtesting.com
Printed in the USA
LVIW01n2247090916
503995LV00002B/5